Unconditional *Flows*

Unconditional Flows

These Are the Favorites Too

KASEY C. JONES

authorHOUSE®

AuthorHouse™ LLC
1663 Liberty Drive
Bloomington, IN 47403
www.authorhouse.com
Phone: 1-800-839-8640

Published by AuthorHouse 09/09/2014

ISBN: 978-1-4969-3868-8 (sc)
ISBN: 978-1-4969-3887-9 (e)

Library of Congress Control Number: 2014916204

Contents

Age Is A Number . . .

Chaff Driven By The Wind

Age Of Chaff

Utter Above My Breath *(revised version)*
That Promise *(revised version)*
An Energy Of People *(revised version)*
The Skies Wing *(revised version)*
Atavistic Cannons *(revised version)*
I'm Better Than Schemes *(revised version)*
Aeon Stories *(revised version)*

Neeu I'm So Proud Of You

I'm proud of you Neeu
Attempting to soar at life
Releasing incorrections in your mind,
Determining which paths has less upheavals.
And Neeu, yes I'm proud
I am proud of you.

Rat, Squirrel

Squirrel is your middle name,
Rat is my middle name but our
first names are the same. I guess
that since we both are adopted our
caretakers or parent/guardians quickly
identified the similarities we share.

Dear Squirrel, I'm glad to be the
student, teacher, in your life.

Dear Rat, I'm glad to be the teacher,
student, in your life.

Claustrophobic

Another large metal door at the
Far end of the chamber.

Towards the beginning I did not
Appreciate people asking me
Questions that are personal but as
I grew I realized I could open their
Minds and clean the dust from my brain.

I once avoided life and closed the doors
To hide away, I even painted pictures
Of what I should've been. This was not
Incorrect however, it was more like a
Dream that seemed better than reality.

Hidden Fronts

The face of a building, to warn
against something. The idea that
everything has symbolic natures, edible
currents that we call simply sightseeing.

Tapestry Wall Hangings

A deerfly took the kettle off the stove
Her peculiar green eyes I could not loathe.

My bones once ached from rocking her
Limp toes. Until that morning I had
Never seen flickers in her eyes growing
Strong and old.

As a deerfly she was never going to
Leave me alone without laying in the
Swelling flood of my passion mold.

Through The Clouds And The Trees

As reckoned from an
Arbitrary past
Point on the continuum,
Roaming clouds are there
Swathing and surmounts our
Potential opposition.

I ascertain in a scene from an upward
Position, just slit timorous to the touch,
At the mercy of a white depleting
Overcoat.

Or to another
Person I esteem
Too greatly in mist.

Young Vocabulary

The baby heard my voice and turned
Around as if an echo warmed its ears
Continuously.

I'd gone back into a slight sleep
And you'd have thought that the mother of
That baby had slipped me some of her milk.
Anyway, it had been a dream filled with
Horizons and a beach smoothing over
Waves and shoulders of sand.

When I awoke there was nothing in front
Of me, the little one had gone and for a
Minute I felt as if I'd lost my own kid.

I'd saw the baby lift its fingers at me,
Watching in a colorless fashion and I
Hated that I never heard a crisp
Good-bye from such young squelch
And innocence.
But as the coolness of the mother lingered
I could at least wish for another moment.

Water On My Jeans

A bicycling speed without care to
be uneasy about puddles that
loom my path at times.
I am not shrinking in what appears
A rainforest, my wheels growingly
Whistle to me, I am not afraid.
Quickly goes pedals and fee pushing energy
To steady my destination or what
I already know of it.
Splash, higher, my intrigue like that
Puddle-water trying to match the level of
my jeans. I will be meeting my friends and
family just the way that I am.

Dates

Let me hurry my hirsute head
I'm late for a horrendously ate date.
Tell me, won't upset waging war teacher
And my shiny shrill grades
That sleep in my bed and run to shun
Whenever I fail a test.

I manage relationships and make notes
About them like dates. These dates that
Make me question myself and their motives.

Dates are healthy I'm sure they lower
Your blood pressure, and I'm slower, less, less
Frequently are my dates taking me to lunch.
I'm learning to love myself before I take a bite.

I manage multiple appointments, just dates
That hover over my calendar with Doctors
Smiling because I'm choosing progress.

Fire In The Ink (revised version)

Coming to destroy my page in the realm,
Warding to greaten their rage does jury,
Evolving to collect a day screaming unsatisfiable
Greed. Rampant does rainstorms and the fowl
To the ink scribbles pernicious burns that sway
To and from form. Look closer, up the tools,
If not center for be it all a signature that we
Share in creation, it is our power, people placed
Clearly in ordeals; structure: to every thought,
For every letter, there is a story. Own your
Dilapidated mental gears so that all inclines ere
This progress and a rainbow incinerates its
Expense. Dervish speaks; Tsunamis in his mouth
And as iron at the places of our atom, his
Beliefs eat its falsehood while we drown
Some sickening in the grand script we read.

Intent

Could you sit down please?
I just have one question.

What are they for?

They give me a feeling,
They give me a something, a feeling
That exists in the same world
As happiness.
I store them and I am proud.
I do not agree with any regulations
And I take every opportunity to
Regulate the government.
I'm sure you think I'm shallow,
I'm often seen as insecure
And worrisome but now let me
Ask you a question also.

Does it matter how big a flaw is?
I think I'll stand up.

Don't Always Expect Unconditional . . .

In a web, our lines connect
As we seem to depend on each
Other for support and we at
Points fail to respect and show
Consideration for the hidden
Attributes of each individual line.

Coconuts

Her weather is temperament,
Slices of mint chocolate and coconuts
Sweetened by something.

Drifting to some land for a journey,
A person or a purpose and all of the above.

My rounds are creamy with a hint
Of salt, or so I've been told, I
Sit on a smooth fluid. I love
To make and take orders that drain
My beauty and yet ends their hunger
Or thirst for them to be back again.

Better

The day is as loyal as the night and
These times are just as royal as you might
Like. We rent elaborate adornment
As things we love to replace because we
Are focused and we prefer these costumes
To serve us better right.

We'll lead better if we aren't so
Clear, clear as crystal or wasteful
Plastic thin to the touch. You are
Regal, I tend to splendid and I
Know that we would like to only be
Magnificent, magnificent lunch to
Our eyes when possibly just simply
Meaningful is often not close enough.

Roads I'll Take With Me

Now I inhale the red wine, shaded
Winding roads.

I'm accepting of my peace, the
Kind you have in cruise ship suites
And morning walks with the dog.

I'll be appreciating music for as long
As it soothes. I know that
Quality in it is easily skewed.

I embrace movement whenever it is in
Your body or in my singing voice
And in your call to me.

I'll always remember my colors, collages
Of various nuances and portraits.

These nicely amongst the roads I'll take
With me.

It Was Reported

The hours are hourly.
The masters might subtract mastery.
The connoisseurs may forget what is purely.
The authors do things popularly.
The hungers last to prove hungry.

Hurts

If I must think about the next time
You'll be hurt, I would say don't
Opt to moan or cry. Go into
The outside of those four walls
And if you are already out there
Wait a moment to realize the
Careless whispers of things and beings
And messages they hint to you.

If I must think about the next time
You'll be hurt, I would say do collect
Yourself and try counting poems that
Remind you of the changing weather
And how birds seem to rest their
Wings at times only to start a completely
New flight from the one just flown and
Some fly in groups, others fly in lines.

Notes

Notes, cool even to think. Not only
Slow, refreshing but warm and more
Bold notes I'll share for another person,
Another moment and another date.
Do these leave remnants? And are
They like marbles? Stones, in your
Mind that were always available to
Use, real as mathematics. Or could
They be somewhat intangible or even
A mixture of both depending on the
Subject and who gives a care.

Notes cool even to think.

For Some, Want Snack Box Inside

For some random reason, I noticed
The letters on your sleek cellphone.

It's glossy and black,
Resting on a black computer table and sweet
Snack box.

9 numbers on the keypad. Black buttons
With white markings on the inside.

While being at a loss for words, those
Buttons can text you what you
Want very quickly.

Might you get lost in all of the
Sentences that you send,
I hope that you're not driving.

It Was Stony

It was stony to hide worries from
Them of course, that is what
You'd prefer me to stay, possibly.
I did not plan to be so careful
And feeling responsible for the
Chain of things that happened like
Well attended parties and everyone
There was actually me.

Utter Above My Breath (revised version)

I am a soldier, one that
Cannot be destroyed,
A great many will follow after me.
I am the
Thunderous applause
To the earth
Appreciating the teardrops
That may show sadness on
My face.
I am sugar in benevolence
Providing a good day
That has no hurry.

I am a blending moon
That runs like the sun.
I am in the stretching sky
When the earth grows quiet.

Ladders (revised version)

I lift a man, I hand a prose, I speak a firm voice tone,
I amaze myself in bits working a step,
You smell a rose, you charm a shy, figure unknown and
Spouse.
You create obstacles for priests among ease.

She picks up a man, he makes land but I
Am calm as is all of me including this ladder high,
My ladder, my embrace to these people down,
I seem deep when you lose focus
and leave the answer key.

At the end I am your intuition,
And wisdom that peered just at each level.
At the end I am pure confidence, and
Positive attitude that never fails.
At the end I am sense because you won't leave me.

That Promise (revised version)

I dropped a promise that went all the way back to some
Night.
I dropped long pieces of escape concerning one.
I dropped finally out of their music that never
Really went away.
I dropped, stopped and tapped to
the sound of nothingness.
And starting my truck I took that promise and I
Reexamined it.

I dropped from fear to visit confidence when such a vow
Would place passed my feet,

But never did I affect its presence, I could
Only move, and failing to notice fear;
Anxiety strapped it to me.

I dropped somewhere here and
Over there began to come for me. I embraced
Whatever it was that came to me and
I promised to remember.

An Energy Of People (revised version)

In that strange light all distance died.
You know the world's intensity.

No one can stop for too long, all is
Not seemingly worth a heavy dime
Because first a hesitant heart looks
Like it will get everything through it.

These nuances are in my path, past
Silence, the toad's asthmatic breath
Is pain, the cutworm's tooth grinds and
Grates, and the root, in earth screams, screams

Screams again.

The Skies Wing (revised version)

The tightened sunlight once rolled soft
Strong rays hung on siblings' mere cough,
And warmed their stolen loft; pleading
That backwards eavesdrop the skies wing.
The draw of breezes just precious
From eerie peace found suspicious
Unhinges a trace novel fact.
Relatively thin in the act,
The space between philosophies
To front surprise theosophy.
This is how the shies wing.

Atavistic Cannons (revised version)

Today I think
Only with scents, scents dead leaves yield,
And bracken, and carrots seed,
And the square mustard field;

Windows that rise
When the skulls appear to be a towering tree,
I peek out of my warm body
Dreams, visions, gold honey;

And so smell dies
So I reject the bonfire but taste
The power of my mind, calling
The dead here to waste.

It is enough
To look, to crumble the dark earth,
While the robin sings over again
Sad songs of autumn mirth.

Today I think that
Windows will rise and
For some smell, will
Come alive and that will be enough.

I'm Better Than Schemes
(revised version)

Turning on a furnace I then hugged a flame
Raging, through the grapes and plenty I kindle,
Explosive came a temper for a small me
Panting with what nourishment I called mine whole;
The poorest of my kind has better than schemes.

Up against the belly I feed, at salute stands dissipated
Clouds, lying resemble, most trees and cool clowns.
As I walked these balls of vision swam intricate in earth
Settings,
Sleeping over the imperfections; stars down.

And when dirt is wet I grab my skates, I'm better
Than schemes.

Aeon Stories (revised version)

Drink. I want to drink in your stories.
I'll tuck away the rivers that awoke my
Soul deeper into your, a sacred place just
Like mine, we are divine. I want many
Fluid lessons that withstand the strongest
Drain that could ever happen. This time
I'll take the quietest weeping to only
Transform it across all sorrow,
Instructing it, lying near it, speaking kind
To it. Yes. I want to drink in your stories
And show them beautifully back to you.
A dream with joy and aeon music ending.